RELIGION

CULTURE ENCYCLOPEDIA

RELIGION

Fiona MacDonald

Mason Crest

Mason Crest Publishers Inc.
370 Reed Road
Broomall, PA 19008
(866) MCP-BOOK (toll free)
www.masoncrest.com
This edition first published in 2003

First published by Miles Kelly Publishing,
Bardfield Centre, Great Bardfield, Essex, CM7 4SL, U.K.
Copyright © Miles Kelly Publishing 2002, 2003

2 4 6 8 10 9 7 5 3 1

Library of Congress Cataloging-in-Publication Data on file
at the Library of Congress

ISBN 1-59084-482-3

Author
Fiona MacDonald

Designed and Edited by
Starry Dog Books

Project Editor
Belinda Gallagher

Assistant Editors
Mark Darling, Nicola Jessop, Isla Macuish

Artwork Commissioning
Lesley Cartlidge

Indexer
Jane Parker

Picture Research
Ruth Boardman, Liberty Newton

Color Reproduction
DPI Colour, Saffron Walden, Essex, UK

Printed in China

Contents

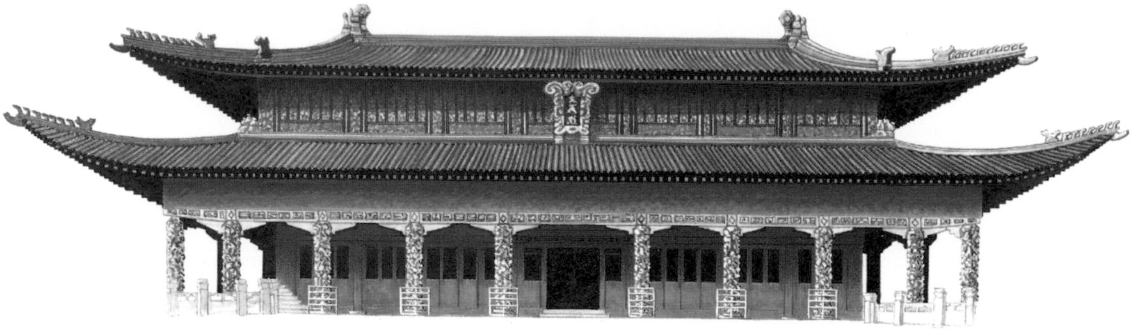

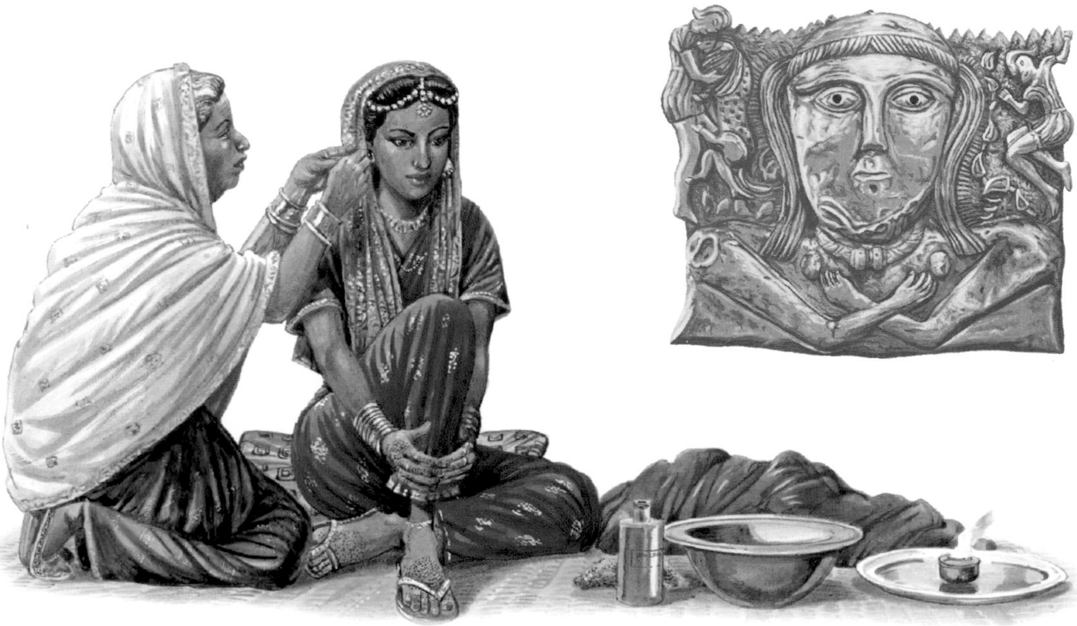

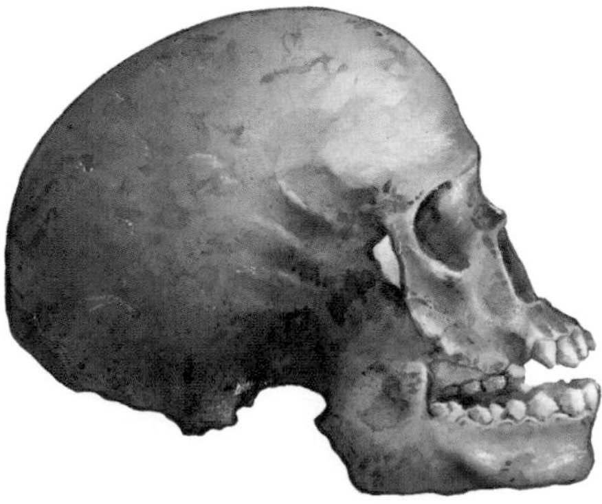

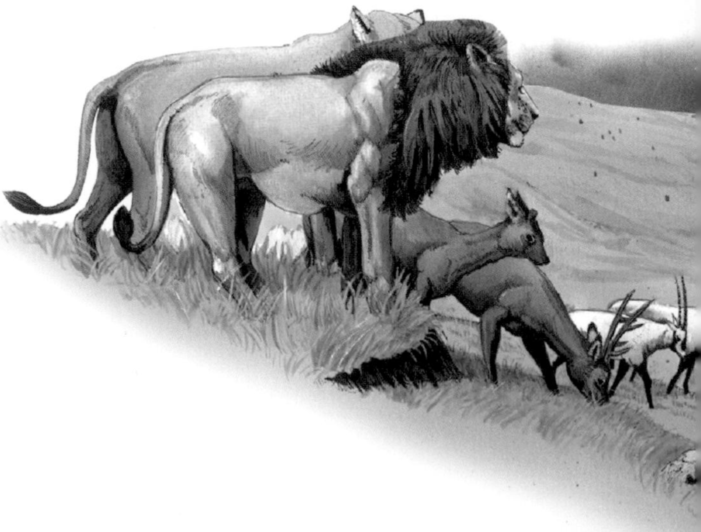

Religion

RELIGION is a way of making sense of the world. It can give people meaning and purpose to their lives, and provide hope of continued existence after death. Many religions make laws encouraging good behavior, but religious disagreements have also led to wars. No one is sure when religious beliefs began, but many archaeologists suggest they may have originated with the first languages about two million years ago. Once early humans had learned to communicate practical needs, it was probably not long before they were able to express deeper feelings and religious ideas.

Seeking God

RELIGIOUS experiences are some of the most powerful known to humankind. They can range from visions of divine beings to a sense of inner peace. Over the centuries, they have inspired believers to perform acts of heroism and compassion—but they have also sparked bitter wars. People seek to make contact with their God, or gods, in different ways. Some go on pilgrimage to holy places; some meditate on the wonders of the world. Others use the teachings of their faith in their lives. In this way, the smallest action becomes a religious experience, and a way of showing devotion to God.

◣ OUT OF THIS WORLD

The world can be a magical, mysterious place, and human feelings can be so powerful that it seems impossible for them to disappear completely at death. Many religions teach that after death our souls live on outside the body, finding eternal peace with God.

LIVING BY FAITH

In the past, most people had religious faith. They relied on religion to explain life's mysteries. Today, many people choose to rely on scientific knowledge. But many people still believe in the soul, or spirit, which science still cannot fully explain.

◨ HOLY PLACES

Almost all religions have special holy places, where priests hold rituals and make offerings and where worshipers can pray and ask for help from their gods. This Chinese temple is decorated with prayers written in red and gold. In China, these are the traditional colors of good luck and blessings.

靈客堂

☑ A MESSAGE FROM GOD?

Since ancient times, people all around the world have interpreted dramatic natural events, such as storms and sunsets, as messages from the gods. Some religions honor nature gods, who control the sun, moon, winds, waves, and weather. Others worship one great creator-God, maker and sustainer of the whole universe.

▷ AWE AND WONDER

The beauty of the natural world, including delicate creatures like this butterfly, have inspired countless people with feelings of awe and wonder. Religious teachers from many faiths encourage their followers to respect the natural environment. They ask us to honor and respect all living things, because they believe them to be made by God.

☑ SYMBOLS OF FAITH

Sacred symbols are used to identify members of different faiths. A six-pointed star was used as a seal by Jewish King David (ruled c.1010–970 BC). Today, a blue Star of David forms part of the Israeli national flag.

▷ A GRAND DESIGN?

For thousands of years, religious people have asked questions such as "why was I born?" and "what is the meaning of life?" Seeing plants and animals living in carefully balanced ecosystems makes us wonder whether we also form part of a grand design. Is human existence planned and guided by God, or are we free to think and act as we choose?

Mystery and magic

THE details of early religions have not survived. But we can still detect traces of them today among peoples who live like the first humans, as hunters and gatherers—for example, in the Amazon rainforests of South America. For early humans, it seems that the world was full of mystery and magic. It was a holy place, in which gods, humans, and the whole natural environment were closely linked together and were dependent on one another. Everything—men, women, plants, rocks, animals, and even the weather—had a spirit or soul that must be honored. Many early peoples also believed in a supreme god and in other supernatural beings.

◄ BURIED WITH CARE

This human skull was buried in the Grimaldi Caves in Italy about 28,000 years ago. It was decorated with red ocher, a paint made from red earth. The decoration was probably a sign of honor or respect, and may indicate that the people who buried the skull believed in life after death.

◄ PROTECTIVE MAGIC

The Celtic civilization flourished in many parts of Europe from about 800 BC to AD 100. This Celtic warrior's skin and shield are painted with magic and sacred designs. The Celts believed that religion and magic could help protect them in battle.

◄ SHARING SPIRIT POWER

Magnificent cave paintings like this one of a bison were painted on the walls of a cave at Lascaux in southern France about 17,000 years ago, and hundreds of similar paintings were found in caves nearby. The pictures were probably created to honor the spirits of wild animals. Early people may have used them in religious rituals.

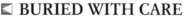

LIFE AFTER DEATH

People from many civilizations—from South America to Siberia—have aimed to help people's spirits survive by carefully preserving their dead bodies. But the best-known examples of this religious custom are probably Egyptian mummies (left).

◰ PAST AND PRESENT

This 19th-century painting of Australian Aboriginals records a ceremony called a corroboree that originated many thousands of years ago. By singing and dancing, the people called on sacred spirits to help their community and make it strong. Aboriginals still preserve many ancient traditions, including religious rituals.

◰ IN HARMONY WITH NATURE

Traditionally, native peoples of North and South America believed that the natural and supernatural worlds were closely linked. They honored many "holy" places, where they believed they could make contact with gods and spirits, and they prayed to natural forces such as the wind and rain to help them survive.

◪ MYSTERIOUS MONUMENT

The stone-passage grave at Newgrange in Ireland was built about 3100 BC. The tomb builders deliberately positioned the round doorway so that it would channel the sun's rays into the burial chamber just once a year, at midwinter. This may have had some religious meaning, but no written evidence has survived to tell us what it might be.

Ancestor spirits

TRADITIONAL religions taught that spirits of dead ancestors continued to play an important part in the world. They possessed (took over) family members, who fell into a trance and spoke with the spirit's voice. They offered advice or warnings, and made demands. Believers thought that the spirits within them had the power to heal or harm. They tried to please ancestor spirits by building shrines where they could "feed" them with food, water, or blood. They summoned them through rituals and dances, then, when the spirits' work was done, performed exorcisms (special ceremonies) to drive them away.

◨ ROYAL REVERENCE

In the ancient kingdom of Benin in West Africa, beautiful brass and bronze altar-statues were made to commemorate dead kings. People believed that the spirits of dead kings could survive in the hearts and minds of rulers that were still alive.

◪ ANCESTOR STORY

This dancer from the Aranda Aboriginal people of central Australia is retelling an ancient myth. It describes how his ancestors fought against two man-eating eagles that attacked his tribe. He is wearing strings of eagle feathers, and a feathered headdress. The bunches of leaves he is holding represent an eagle's wings.

◩ THE POWER OF THE DEAD

Traditionally, the Hemba people of Zaire carved wooden statues, called *singiti*, of their dead ancestors. They believed that by offering the statues food and prayers, they could connect with their ancestors' spirits, and that this would give them power to heal illness or help hunters find food.

HALLOWEEN

In Christian Europe and North America, children celebrate Halloween (the night before All Saints' Day) by dressing up as witches and making ghostly pumpkin lanterns. In the past, people believed that the spirits of the dead left their graves at Halloween to wander.

◄ MEN OR MONSTERS?

Square, bronze containers made in ancient China more than 3,000 years ago held food and drink offered as sacrifices to ancestor spirits. The vessels were decorated with faces of *taotie*—fierce monsters with claws and horns. Historians think that *taotie* originated as pictures of male ancestors, but that over the years the human faces began to be portrayed as monsters—probably, because early people feared that ancestor spirits might haunt them or do them harm.

◄ ANCESTOR GIFTS

The traditional faith of Japan is called Shinto (the Way of the Gods). Followers worship nature spirits, and also the spirits of dead ancestors, which they believe can protect them. Shinto priests hold rituals to please ancestor spirits, and light lanterns and make offerings at holy shrines. Today, favorite gifts include flowers and *sake* (rice wine).

◄ TALL TOTEM

"Totems" are spirit helpers. They can be special animals with magic powers, or the spirits of dead ancestors, shamans, and heroes. Native Americans from northwestern North America shape the trunks of tall trees into towering totem poles that stand outside the homes of high-ranking families. Each pole tells the history of a particular family, commemorating brave deeds by dead ancestors, or stories and legends about family members. They may also portray the family's special totem animal, such as this huge eagle.

Shamans and sacrifices

OVER the centuries, one of the most important religious questions people have asked is "how can we make contact with our gods?" In northeast Asia and the Americas, magicians and healers known as shamans were able to enter a strange state of mind—by chanting, fasting, or sometimes taking powerful herbs—in which they felt like they were flying through the air or diving deep underground. They believed these disturbing experiences allowed them to leave their bodies and enter the land of the spirits. There, traditionally, the shamans learned valuable new knowledge, fought with evil forces, and spoke to the gods. People also tried to make contact with their gods by offering them gifts or sacrifices. They hoped the gods would send them blessings in return.

◢ SEEKING SPIRITS

Shamans asked sacred spirits to make sure the seasons arrived on time, and that there was enough food for families to survive. This shaman from Mongolia is carrying a drum, for summoning spirits and lulling humans into a trance.

◿ SELF – SACRIFICE

Viking legends told how Odin, the shaman god of wisdom, sought knowledge by sacrificing himself to himself. For nine days and nights, he hung in agony from the branches of an ash tree, until he had learned magic secrets. Like other shamans, he had spirit-helpers—two ravens, called Thought and Memory, who flew beside him wherever he went.

◳ IN DISGUISE

Sometimes shamans disguise themselves to help them pass more easily into the spirit world. At other times, they put on disguises to embody powerful nature spirits, or to act out the events they want to make happen. This shaman from the Asmat region of Africa is wearing an elaborate spirit mask that covers him from head to foot.

LIFE AND POWER

The Aztecs, who were powerful in Central America from AD 1300–1521, believed that they had to "feed" their gods, or else the world would end. They sacrificed captives at pyramid-temples, letting their blood flow down the steps.

◄ SHARING ANIMAL POWER

This North American shaman, painted during the 19th century, is wearing furs and feathers taken from powerful wild animals such as bears and eagles. Shamans believed they could draw strength from such animals—their spirit ancestors—and that this would help protect them in the dangerous spirit world.

► LIVING SPIRIT

Followers of many traditional beliefs often make models to represent the spirits they honor, or to act as homes for the spirits if they visit Earth. This kachina, or spirit-figure, was made by the Hopi people of North America. The Hopi honor the spirits of the sun, winds, rain, and corn plants (their traditional staple food).

◄ HEALING POWERS

In many communities, shamans serve as counselors and healers. People who are unwell consult them because they believe their illness is caused by evil spirits, and that the shaman has power to drive them away. Shamans, like this traditional healer from Africa, may use songs and rattles to frighten the spirits, or other "magical" curing aids, such as bones and stones.

Nature gods

ABOUT 8000 BC, for the first time, people began to live as farmers in settled villages, rather than roaming the land as hunter gatherers. They grew plants and kept animals for food. This changed lifestyle led to the development of new religious beliefs. People began to think of Earth as their kindly, generous mother, and to honor the sun, wind, and weather— together with important food plants —as gods and goddesses who controlled the natural world. If the crops withered or the rains failed, communities were struck by famine and many people died. So, at important seasons of the farming year, they made offerings and sacrifices to please all the different nature gods.

◩ **SPIRIT OF THE RAIN**
In ancient Japan, froglike nature spirits called Kami were believed to control the rain, winds, and storms. According to Shinto—the traditional religion of Japan—Kami control all natural forces. They can be kind and gentle or fierce and very dangerous.

◪ **HIDDEN AMONG TREES**
Once families had settled in villages, woodland became a place of fear. In England, villagers dreaded meeting the Green Man—a sinister nature god who lived in the trees.

◩ **POWER OVER NATURE**
Many peoples used religious rituals and magic ceremonies to try to win influence over the natural world. Native Americans performed ritual dances, with the aim of attracting buffalo to the hunting grounds close to their villages or tipi camps. Young men in buffalo costumes danced day and night, until lookouts announced that buffalo had been sighted. The buffalo were then killed for food and their skins.

◢ GUNDESTROP BOWL

Celtic civilization flourished throughout Europe from about 800 BC to AD 100. The Celts worshiped many nature gods, and also blended their own religious ideas with earlier traditions and with the beliefs of peoples living nearby. This goddess was pictured on a famous piece of Celtic metalwork, the Gundestrop bowl, which was made in eastern Europe.

◣ LORD OF THE LIFE-GIVING RAIN

Food crops, such as wheat in the Middle East and corn in Central America, were so important for early farmers that they became like gods. The life-giving rain that helped them grow was also worshiped. This clay statue, made between AD 600–900, portrays a rain god honored by the Maya people, who lived in the rainforests of Central America.

SHINING SUN GOD

The Inca people, who lived in the Andes mountains of Peru (AD 1100s–1532), worshiped Inti, the golden god of the sun. He brought light and warmth every day, protecting the Inca and helping their crops to grow.

◢ GOD OF THUNDER

Early farmers dreaded thunderstorms, which could flatten their crops and wipe out the harvest. Many worshiped gods who they believed controlled thunder, like Thor, the mighty Viking god of storms. Legend tells how Thor rode through the clouds in his chariot, brandishing a great thunderbolt.

Gods, heroes, and kings

BY ABOUT 3500 BC, some villages had grown into the first cities, ruled by powerful kings. City dwellers practiced many new skills—there were weavers and potters, metal workers, soldiers, merchants, and tax collectors. New forms of religion developed to meet the people's needs. They worshiped their city's unique guardian god, or the gods and goddesses who protected their special craft. In ancient Egypt and the Middle East, the people believed that kings, queens, and local heroes were divine. All these gods were worshiped in new kinds of buildings—huge temples, designed as holy homes for them, where they were served by priests.

◣ LION-KILLER

The ancient Greek hero Hercules (son of Zeus, king of the gods) was said to be "superhuman." He performed twelve dangerous "labors," or tasks, one of which was killing the Nemean Lion—a man-eating monster. After completing his labors, the gods rewarded him with immortality.

◪ GOD, PRIEST, OR KING?

This statue of a dignified bearded man was found in the ruined city of Mohenjo-Daro, in the Indus Valley (in the far northwest of the Indian subcontinent). It was made about 2200 BC by the rich and technologically advanced civilization that flourished there. The statue is thought to portray either a god, a priest, or a king—or perhaps a powerful man who was honored as all of these. We cannot tell for certain, because no one has yet been able to decipher the mysterious system of writing used by scribes of the Indus Valley culture.

HERO-KING

Gilgamesh, king of the city of Etrech, features in many myths and legends from the ancient Middle East. Some are more than 4,000 years old. He was said to be two-thirds god, one third man.

☑ HOLY KNOWLEDGE

Writing, which developed in many parts of the world after about 3000 BC, enabled religious ideas and stories to be recorded permanently. For many centuries only a few well-educated people (usually priests) knew how to read and write. This is a scribe from the Mayan civilization of Central America.

☑ SEAT OF POWER

This wood carving shows a Yoruba king from West Africa. Traditionally, the Yoruba people worshiped many different gods, including Olorun (Lord of the Sky), orishas (life-giving forces), ancestors, and nature spirits. Many Yoruba kings claimed kinship with the orishas.

◪ EGYPTIAN OFFERINGS

The ancient Egyptians believed that their kings, whom they called pharaohs, were the children of gods—especially the sun god Amun-Ra and the cow-headed mother goddess Hathor. Half-human, half-divine, the pharaohs formed a living link between the gods and ordinary people.

◪ CHOSEN BY GOD

Many groups of people, as well as individuals, have believed that they were specially chosen by God. He was their special protector and savior. If they worshiped Him and obeyed His laws, He would take care of them. The Bible tells the story of Noah, who obeyed God's command to build an ark, or large ship, in which to house his family and one pair of all the animals in the world. God then sent a great flood to punish the world. Only Noah, his family, and the animals survived.

Hindus and Sikhs

HINDUISM is the religion of India. It originated about 1500 BC among the Aryan people of the northwest. About 1000 BC, the first Hindu holy books, the *Vedas*, were written down. These describe the gods and goddesses and record hymns and prayers. Since then, Hinduism has divided into many sects, but its essential beliefs remain the same. Hindus aim to escape from this world and unite their souls with Brahman by following *dharma* (the right way to live). Until they lead pure lives, Hindus believe they will be reborn in different bodies again and again. The Sikh faith was founded in 1499 by a Hindu named Guru Nanak. He believed that people were all children of the same god, and preached religious tolerance.

◄ TEMPLES
Many Hindus go to a *mandir*, or temple, to say prayers and make offerings of sweets and flowers. The temples are often beautifully decorated with carvings of gods and spirits. The name for a holy statue that represents a favorite goddess or god is a *murti*.

▶ SIKH HOLY SHRINE
The Golden Temple, or *Harimandar*, at Amritsar in India is built on the ground where Guru Nanak spent time meditating about God. It is a specially holy place for Sikhs.

◄ THE RIVER OF HEAVEN
To Hindus, the River Ganges, which flows through the city of Varanasi, is specially sacred. They call it the "River of Heaven." Hindus make pilgrimages to its banks to pray and worship. They also cremate, or burn, the bodies of the dead there, so that the dead person's soul—free from its body—can continue on its spiritual journey.

☑ LIFE CYCLES

Like people from many different religions, Hindu familes mark important stages in each individual's life, such as weddings (below) and funerals, with prayers and religious ceremonies. They also believe that ordinary, everyday actions have a religious meaning. Each good deed takes a person closer to his or her spiritual goal, which is freedom from life in this world and union with Brahman, the supreme God.

SIKH SIGNS

Sikhs wear five special things to show their faith:
Kes = uncut hair
Kirpan = a small sword
Kara = a steel bangle
Kanga = a wooden comb
Kacch = white shorts

▭ HINDU PRIEST

Hindu priests come from the highest caste, or rank, within Hindu society –they are Brahmins. There are also many Hindu spiritual teachers, or gurus. Priests and gurus teach important Hindu beliefs, including *dharma* (the right way to live), reincarnation (the soul's rebirth in a new body after death), and *karma* (the law of spiritual punishment and reward).

◸ CELEBRATING THE SEASONS

Like people from many other faiths, Hindus hold festivals to celebrate the changing seasons. Holi is a spring festival held in February or March. On the first day, people light bonfires. On the second day, they honor the playful god Krishna by playing practical jokes, such as throwing colored powders or colored water.

The way of Buddha

BUDDHA, or the Enlightened One, was the name given to Siddhartha Gautama, an Indian prince who lived from about 560 to 480 BC. As a young man, he set out to travel the world, and was horrified to see so much suffering. Seeking to find a reason for it, he spent years meditating under a holy tree. People came to listen to his spiritual teaching and to ask his advice. The Buddha taught Four Noble Truths: 1) suffering is always part of life; 2) it is caused by greed or desire; 3) suffering (and life itself) will end when believers achieve *Nirvana* (perfect peace); and 4) *Nirvana* can be found by following the Eightfold Path of Buddhist study, prayer, and meditation. After the Buddha's death, his followers traveled throughout Southeast Asia spreading the news of his teachings in many lands.

◢ BUDDHIST MONK

Many Buddhist men and women decide to spend some time as monks or nuns, to learn more about their faith. This *bhikkhu*, or Buddhist monk, is studying holy scriptures.

◿ BOROBODUR

About AD 800, this huge center of Buddhist worship was built at Borobodur on the island of Java, in Indonesia. It is the largest Buddhist holy building in the world. Six square terraces surround a central shrine. The walls of the lower terraces are covered with beautiful carvings portraying different aspects of the spiritual world.

◁ PALACE AND FORTRESS

Originally built as a fortress during the Middle Ages, the massive Potala Palace became the home of the Dalai Lamas, leaders of Buddhists in Tibet, during the 17th century. In 1959, the present Dalai Lama left the palace to live in India after Chinese troops took control of Tibetan lands.

☑ A GUIDE FOR LIFE

Buddhists do not worship the Buddha as a god, but rather honor him as a guide who shows them the best way to live. There are many huge, splendid statues of the Buddha, carved from stone or cast from bronze or even pure gold. Buddhists leave offerings of flowers, incense, and candles beside the statues.

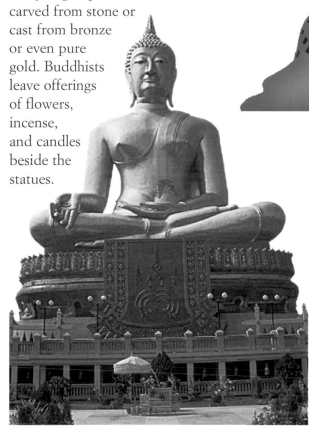

STUPAS

A stupa is a Buddhist monument. The first stupas were built to house the remains of the Buddha's body after he died. Later stupas were built to contain Buddhist holy writings or the bones of respected teachers and monks.

☑ GARDENS FOR MEDITATION

Zen is a type of Buddhism popular in Japan. Its followers believe that meditation is the best way to reach spiritual peace and understanding. A Zen garden is made of raked sand, gravel, and stones, where followers can sit quietly and focus their minds on meditation.

☑ PAGODA IN BURMA

The spread of Buddhist teachings was encouraged by many kings and princes, who supported Buddhist monks and scholars and paid for magnificent Buddhist monuments. This beautiful temple in Burma is one of over 5,000 Buddhist shrines built on the orders of King Anawrahta (ruled 1044–1077) and his descendants. Its tall pagoda towers have many separate layers, each one representing stages in a soul's progress toward *Nirvana*.

Confucius and Laozi

IN CHINA, the two most important religions are Confucianism and Daoism, both of which are based on moral teachings. Confucianism was founded by Kongfuzi, or Confucius (c.551–479 BC). Confucius was not concerned with worshiping gods, or with hopes of life after death. Instead, he taught people to live a good life, encouraging self control, hard work, and respect for families. Daoism is based on the writings (called the *Daodejing*, or The Way) of philosopher Laozi, who lived about the same time as Confucius. Laozi described many gods, nature spirits, and magical practices, and encouraged meditation and spiritual harmony.

◥ WATCHFUL GOD
In China, many people who respect Confucian or Daoist teachings also believe in traditional gods, such as the "Kitchen God." He is believed to watch people as they go about their lives, and he reports wrongdoings to Heaven. His picture is kept in the kitchen.

◁ WISE TEACHER
Kongfuzi, or Confucius, encouraged his followers to be responsible, wise, and modest, and to show kindness and loyalty to others. Many of his wise sayings were written down by people who admired them. Today, millions of people in China and eastern Asia are still guided by his teachings.

▷ RULERS' DUTIES
Chinese emperors built many splendid temples, like this one in the "Forbidden City" in Beijing. They visited the temples to make offerings on behalf of their people, asking the gods to send good harvests, peace, and prosperity. Confucius said that rulers should obey the "will of heaven" by governing wisely and respecting the gods.

▲ RESPECT

Traditionally, younger members of Chinese families show respect for elders, and women show respect for men—Confucius taught that the oldest man in a family was its head and should be obeyed. But mothers and grandmothers often have considerable power within a household, controlling almost everything that happens.

◩ DAOISM

Laozi taught that there is a great power, known as Dao (the Way), that guides the universe. His followers, called Daoists, try to live in harmony with Dao. This can mean living good lives, taking political action, or retreating to a wild place to be close to nature. Daoists use physical exercise and breathing techniques to bring their bodies closer to the life force of Dao.

LIVING IN HARMONY

Daoists believe that the natural world is in a state of balance between two contrasting forces, Yin and Yang. Yin is cold, dark, and female, and Yang is hot, light, and male. They are often represented by this black-and-white circular symbol. By following Dao (the Way), Daoists try to keep these forces in harmony.

◪ A LASTING MEMORIAL

After Confucius died he was honored almost like a god. A temple was built in the city of Qufu, Shandong Province, where he had lived. Prayers were said there, and offerings were made to his spirit. Over the years, Confucius' temple was enlarged and rebuilt by Chinese emperors as a sign of respect, until it became one of the most splendid religious buildings in all China.

Judaism

THE FOLLOWERS of three great religions—Judaism, Christianity, and Islam—are often described as "Peoples of the Book." They all honor the same holy text, known as the Old Testament of the Bible, and respect the prophets, or religious teachers, whose actions are described in it. All three faiths originated in the Middle East, although today they have believers worldwide. Judaism is the oldest—it first developed about 2000 BC. Its followers believe in a single, all-powerful God, who created the world, freed the Jewish people from slavery in Egypt, led them to a Promised Land, known as Israel, and set down laws (or commandments) telling them how to live good lives and set an example to others.

▷ CREATOR GOD

Jewish beliefs have inspired people from many faiths to produce dramatic and beautiful works of art. This painting shows God creating the first man and woman, Adam and Eve. According to Jewish tradition, the whole world and everything in it was created by God in six days. Adam was made from earth, and Eve was made from a rib bone in Adam's side.

☑ SIGNS OF FAITH

Some Jewish men wear special clothes as a sign of their faith. The *kippah* (or *yarmulke*) is a little cap that covers the crown of the head and is worn as a mark of respect for God. For praying, Jewish men may wear a *tallit*, or shawl.

A SCATTERED PEOPLE

For almost 2,000 years, Jewish people were forced to live outside their traditional homeland in the Middle East. Some settled in Europe, but they were often persecuted. During the 19th century, many Jewish people emigrated to the United States, where they hoped to find religious freedom. Today, there is a Jewish state in Israel, and Jewish communities in many parts of the world.

◤ PRAYING AT THE TEMPLE WALL

Jewish people stand to pray at the Western Wall in Jerusalem. This ancient structure is the only remaining part of the Temple in Jerusalem, a very holy place of worship founded by King Solomon almost 3,000 years ago. Jewish people travel from all over the world to pray there.

◀ SAVED BY A MIRACLE

Moses was a Jewish leader who lived about 1200 BC. God told him to lead the Jews out of Egypt. They were chased by Egyptian soldiers, but—according to Jewish scriptures— God parted the waters of the Red Sea so that Moses and the Jews could cross in safety. When the waters ran back, the Egyptians were drowned.

◤ TEACHING

The Jewish scriptures are called the *Tenakh*. They are divided into three parts, the most important of which is the *Torah*, which means "teaching." This Jewish man is reading from the *Torah* in a synagogue. He has covered his head and shoulders to show respect.

◣ MEMORIAL FESTIVAL

Pesach, or Passover, is a Jewish festival held in March or April. It commemorates the time long ago when the Jews escaped from slavery in Egypt. At the beginning of the festival, Jewish families share a joyful meal and take part in a service called *seder*, with scripture readings and songs. Meals at *Pesach* include flatbread and herbs.

Christianity

CHRISTIANITY originated in the Middle East in the first century AD. Jewish people there believed that a religious teacher named Jesus was "the Messiah," a leader who would free them from Roman rule and bring them closer to God. Jesus respected the teachings of the Jewish prophets, but added his own message: the most important thing in life is to love God and to behave well toward other people. He was killed by the Romans as a danger to public order, but Christians believe he came back to life three days later. They also believe that people who follow his teachings will live after death.

◪ THE CHRISTMAS STORY

Christians believe that Jesus was born in a stable in Bethlehem, to Mary, a virgin, and her future husband Joseph, a carpenter. Three wise men, led by a star, traveled from the east to worship Jesus. They gave him gifts of gold, frankincense, and myrrh.

LIGHT IN DARKNESS

At Christingle—a service that looks forward to Jesus' birth at the darkest time of the year—children carry a decorated orange. The orange represents the world, and the candle stands for the "light" (joy and peace) that Jesus brought to the world.

◁ ALONE WITH GOD

From the beginnings of Christianity, some Christian men and women have chosen to retreat to remote places, such as this mountaintop in Greece, so that they can devote their lives to God. There, in monasteries or convents, they spend their lives in prayer and study.

◁ SPREADING THE GOOD NEWS

Over the centuries, missionaries have carried news of the Christian faith—the Gospel—to countries all over the world. The missionaries shown here are preaching to people in India, in about 1850. Many missionaries built schools and hospitals for the people whom they hoped to persuade to become Christians. Today, there are groups of Christians in almost every country.

▷ NEW CHRISTIANS

Crowds of Christian believers belonging to the Zion Church meet for worship in South Africa. In Europe, many people turned away from organized Christian churches during the 20th century. But in Africa many varieties of Christian worship are thriving. The Zion Church has over 7 million members.

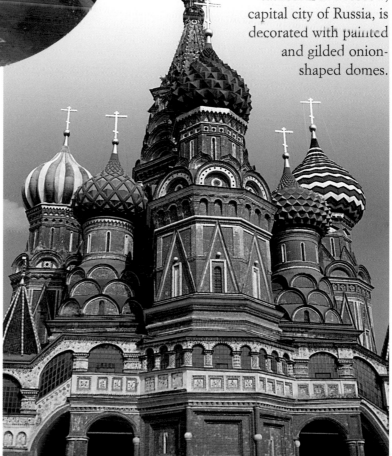

◱ FIT FOR A BISHOP

The Christian Church is led by bishops (senior priests). Each bishop has a home church, called a cathedral. These are often rich, splendid buildings. The cathedral in Moscow, capital city of Russia, is decorated with painted and gilded onion-shaped domes.

◪ A NEW LIFE

Many Christian churches hold a special ceremony, called baptism, to welcome new believers. The person being baptized is sprinkled with water (or sometimes bathed) to show that his or her old life has been washed away and his or her new Christian life has begun. Some churches only baptize adults; others baptize babies. Although a baby is too young to understand the ceremony, its parents and their close friends, chosen to be "godparents," make a promise to bring the child up as a Christian.

Islam

THE FIRST Muslims (believers in Islam) lived in Arabia in the 7th century AD. They were followers of the Prophet Muhammad (c. AD 570–632), a religious teacher who received a series of revelations from God. These were written down to form a holy book, the *Qu'ran*, which is honored as a guide and inspiration by Muslims today. The Prophet Muhammad worshiped a single God, the judge of all human behavior. He also respected earlier Jewish prophets, including Jesus, as being messengers from God. Muslims believe that God will send no more prophets after Muhammad. They obey five rules: 1) belief in God and love for Muhammad; 2) prayer five times a day; 3) fasting during the month of Ramadan; 4) Hajj (pilgrimage to Mecca); and 5) *zakat* (giving to charity).

◀ CALL TO PRAYER

Mosques are buildings where Muslims meet to pray and to listen to readings from their holy book, the *Qu'ran*. They traditionally have at least one tall tower, called a minaret, next to the main building. From a platform at the top, a muezzin—an official with a loud, clear voice—calls Muslims to prayer. In many countries today, the call to prayer is broadcast through loudspeakers.

◤ ACROSS THE DESERT

Muslim traders, scholars, and soldiers traveled long distances across the desert by camel. They carried the faith of Islam with them to many parts of Asia, North and West Africa, and the Middle East.

◤ RELIGIOUS DUTIES

Islam teaches that it is a religious duty to pray five times a day. Muslim men bow down to the ground in prayer, kneeling on a prayer mat. They face in the direction of Mecca, the holy city of Islam.

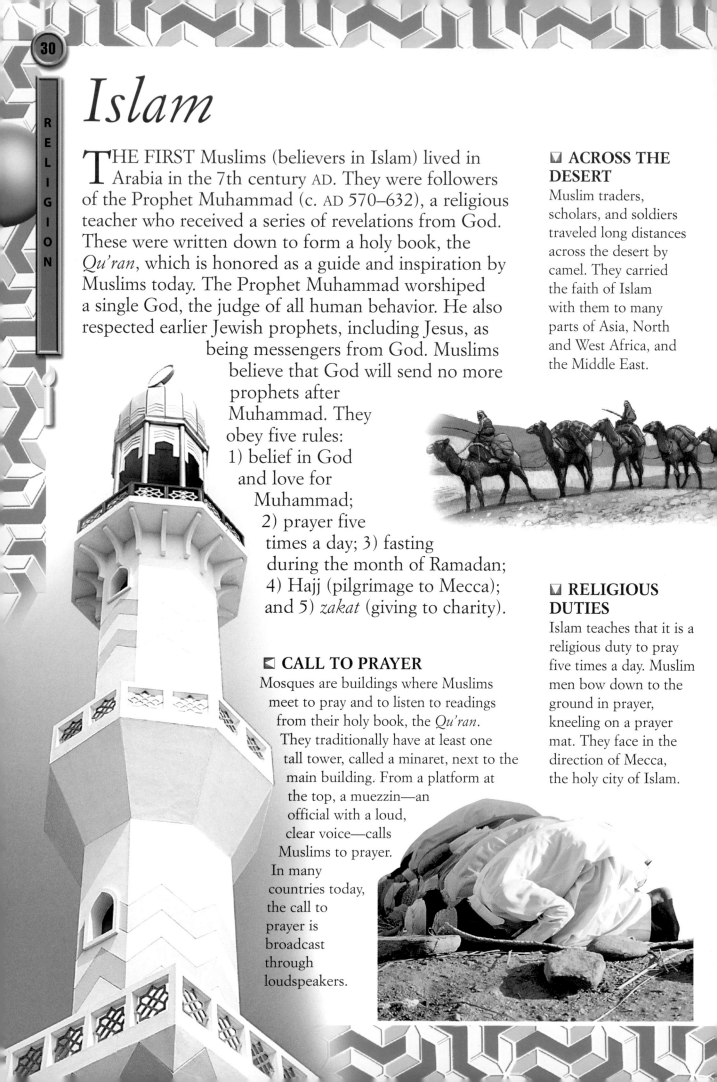

HOLY CITY

For Muslims, Mecca (or Makkah) in Arabia is the most sacred city in the world. At its heart stands the Grand Mosque, containing the Ka'aba—an ancient cube-shaped holy structure draped in black and gold. All Muslims hope to make a pilgrimage to Mecca at least once in their lives.

RELIGIOUS DESIGNS

Muslim craftworkers excel in creating beautiful abstract designs, like the geometric patterns painted on the ceramic tiles that decorate this mosque. Similar designs decorate manuscripts, pottery, and carpets. Islam teaches that it is wrong to make images of living things, since only Allah (God) can create life.

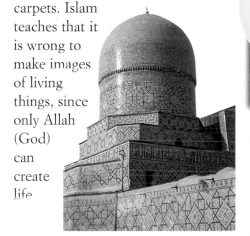

THE MUSLIM CALENDAR

Muslim history starts in AD 622, when Muhammad left Mecca to establish the first Muslim community in Medina. Muslims measure months and years by the moon. Each month has 29 or 30 days.

DOME OF THE ROCK

The Dome of the Rock is a beautiful mosque in Jerusalem, a city (in present-day Israel) that is holy to Muslims, Christians, and Jews. Inside is a large natural rock, from which, Muslims believe, Muhammad made a miraculous night journey to heaven to see Allah (God) on his throne.

New Age

DURING the 20th century, traditional religions became less popular in many parts of the world. Many people stopped believing in God and chose not to go to churches, temples, or other holy places to worship. However, most people did not completely lose their belief in a greater holy power. Some people revived mysterious religions from ancient times, re-creating their rituals. Some invented new religions of their own. Many of these were linked to nature worship, spiritual healing, or faith in pseudo (fake) science. They searched for an alternative lifestyle that would unite mind, body, and spirit, and looked forward to the dawning of a New Age, when men and women would bring peace and love to the universe, and find the god within themselves.

☑ MIND, BODY, AND SPIRIT

Followers of "New Age" philosophies seek to balance mind, body, and spirit. Often they borrow techniques for exercise and meditation from ancient Asian religious traditions. This diagram shows some of the ideas of reiki, a Japanese religious teaching, whose believers aim to live in harmony with the universal life force.

☑ HOLY HERITAGE

The huge stone circle at Stonehenge in southwest England has been a holy site for more than 3,000 years. After centuries of neglect, it has once more become a place of worship. Druids (men and women who re-enact ancient Celtic ceremonies) and people seeking "New Age" spiritual experiences travel there at midsummer to honor the Sun as it rises.

VOICES OF PROTEST

In 1980, in Poland, a group of organized workers (a trade union) called Solidarity was formed. It pressed for changes in the government, and within eight years, the group had 10 million members—too many for the government to overpower. The Polish government eventually had to accept many of Solidarity's demands, and in 1989, Solidarity received a large number of votes in the first free election. This union of people inspired people to strive for more freedom, almost like a religion.

CHURCH AND COMMERCE

In recent times, church leaders have joined a worldwide protest against the way that governments and big businesses control the world economy. They are demanding fair trade deals with people from developing countries, and the cancellation of international debts.

SAVING THE TREES

For many New Age sympathizers, protecting the natural environment from destruction has become a spiritual quest. They hold ceremonies to celebrate nature's beauty, and campaign to save fragile environments, such as rainforests, from harm.

GOOD CAUSES

Traditionally, all the world's faiths have encouraged charity. Increasingly, non religious people also help good causes. In 1984 and 1985, vast concerts raised over £50 million for famine relief in Africa.

A MODERN SAINT?

Diana, Princess of Wales (1961–97), became famous for the work she did to help people who were ill, injured, or outcast. Some people called her a "modern saint," but religious leaders did not approve of this title.

Replacing religion?

IN THE early years of a new millennium, many people are wondering what the future holds for the religions of the world. New scientific discoveries and secular (worldly) political ideas pose a powerful challenge to the power of old beliefs. New causes, such as the Green Movement, provide an alternative to religion for many people. New trends in society, such as individualism and materialism (love of things), mean that consumers look for pleasure and satisfaction here and now, rather than hoping to find peace and joy in a future life, after death. Faced with these challenges, will traditional faiths continue to exist or will they fade away?

◪ CONSUMER PASSIONS
Shopping has been described as the "new religion" of people who seek happiness in material possessions. Many traditional religions encourage people to give up "good things" in the hope of enjoying eternal life in heaven.

▣ PLAYING GOD?
Dolly the sheep was born in Scotland in 1997. Created by scientists using genetic engineering techniques, she was the first mammal to be cloned (copied) from adult cells. Some people fear that scientists are starting to copy God's role of creator.

◪ KNOWLEDGE, NOT FAITH
This amazing photograph, taken through an electron microscope, shows the surface of a tick's skin magnified thousands of times. (A tick is a small bug related to spiders and crabs.) Modern scientific instruments allow us to explore the natural world in great detail. For many people, greater knowledge and understanding of the natural world has replaced their faith in a mysterious, magical God.

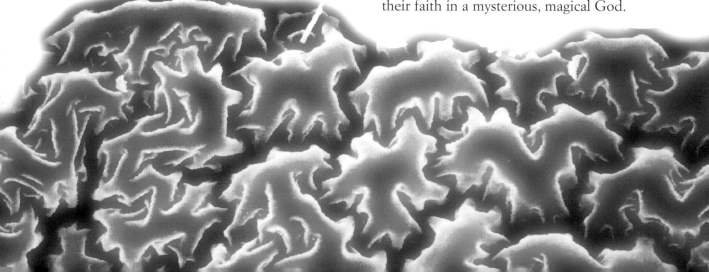

WHO MADE PEOPLE?

The 19th-century biologist Charles Darwin (1809–82) suggested that humans had developed from apes in a natural process called "evolution." At first thought a threat to religion, today his ideas are believed by some people.

◪ **FANATICAL FANS**

In many parts of the world, sports fans follow their teams or the careers of sports superstars with the devotion that people in the past once gave to religion. Their loyalty is to a club and their fellow fans, not to beliefs or religious ideas.

▷ **UNDERSTANDING THE UNIVERSE**

In the late 1990s, supernovas (exploding stars) were photographed by the Hubble space telescope. For centuries, people thought of stars as signs of God's power. Modern space exploration has deepened some people's faith, but it has also increased respect for what human minds can achieve without the help of supernatural powers.

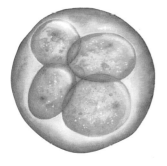

◪ **INTOLERANCE?**

Babies develop from a tiny collection of cells. Many religions teach that babies are gifts from God and should be loved. But in the future, people may demand "perfect" babies, designed by scientists.

Glossary

ALTAR
A large stone, table or similar raised structure at a place of worship, where sacrifices or other offerings are made and prayers are said.

ARCHAEOLOGISTS
Experts who find out how people lived in the past by digging up and studying the places where they lived, and the remains they left behind.

CEREMONY
A special event carried out according to custom or traditional rules, performed to honor and continue some kind of past ritual, rite, or anniversary.

CONVENT
A building where a religious group of women, usually called nuns, live together and devote their lives to worship and prayer.

COUNSELLOR
A person who listens to other people's problems and then tries to give them help, advice and guidance on how best to deal with those problems.

CREMATE
The burning of bodies of dead people on fires called pyres, or in special ovens called crematoria. This reduces the bodies to ashes, which can then be kept or taken to an appropriate place.

DRUIDS
The priests of ancient Celtic religions who especially honored the natural world, in particular oak trees and mistletoe.

ECOSYSTEM
The scientific study of how animals and plants live together and interact in their natural surroundings.

EVOLUTION
A belief that animals and plants change gradually over time by a process called natural selection, and become better suited or adapted to their environment.

EXORCISM
A religious ceremony performed to drive spirits or ghosts away from haunted buildings or places, or out of people's minds, in order to cure illness or treat problems.

FAMINE
A desperate shortage of food, often resulting in disease, starvation, and death.

FANATICS
People whose enthusiasm for something, such as a religion, hobby, or sport, becomes stronger than most ordinary people's, and perhaps begins to cause problems.

FAST
A set period of time during a religious festival when people do not eat, or do not eat certain things.

GENETIC ENGINEERING
When scientists alter the breeding material, or genes, of plants or animals, for reasons such as to cure illness or create new kinds of living things.

GURU
A religious or cultural leader or teacher, especially from the Hindu or Sikh faiths, who gives spiritual guidance.

HALLOWEEN
"All-Hallows Even", the evening before All Saints' Day, which was once called All-Hallows. Some people say that ghosts and spirits are seen on Halloween.

HUNTER GATHERERS
Early humans who hunted animals and gathered fruits, berries and other plant foods, before they learned how to grow crops and domesticate animals.

INCENSE
A gum or resin produced by certain trees which, when burned, produces strongly scented smoke, and is used in religious ceremonies and also to make perfumes.

MAGIC
Apparently mysterious happenings which have no obvious cause other than supposed supernatural means.

MANUSCRIPT
The original handwritten (or more recently, typed) version of a book or document.

MATERIALISM
The interest in acquiring money, obvious wealth, and physical possessions, rather than finding satisfaction in the mind and inner spiritual peace, for example, through following a religion.

MEDITATE
To think very deeply and intently, especially spiritually or religiously. People often sit in special positions or go to special places to meditate.

MISSIONARY
A person who belongs to a particular religion, and who goes to other places to teach, and perhaps convert, others to that religion.

MONASTERY
A building where a religious community of men, usually called monks, live together and devote their lives to worship and prayer.

MOSQUE
A building where Muslims meet to worship, pray, and listen to readings from the Holy Book, the *Qu'ran*.

MUMMIES
Dead bodies from ancient times, which were preserved with chemicals and wrapped in cloth so they would be preserved.

MYRRH
A bitter gum that oozes from the bark of the myrrh tree. It has a strong perfume and was a precious ingredient in incense, medicines and perfumes.

NIRVANA
A state of perfect peace and tranquillity, free from all desire and pain, especially in the Hindu and Buddhist faiths.

PAGODA
A temple tower with many roofed layers or tiers. Originally, each tier represented a stage in the progress of a spirit or soul towards nirvana.

PERSECUTE
To mistreat or harm in some way by others because they are different, for example, if they follow a different religion.

PILGRIMAGE
A journey made by a religious person to an important shrine or holy place, to pray or to worship.

PROPHET
A religious person who speaks words that he or she believes are divine or from his or her god. Prophets tell people what has happened, what will happen, and what their god wants of them.

PYRAMID
A structure with straight-edged base and sloping sides, and which was usually used for religious purposes, such as the tombs of god-kings or pharaohs in Egypt, or sacrifices in the Americas.

REINCARNATION
The belief that when a body dies, its soul moves to, or is reborn, somewhere else—perhaps in another body. The new body may be a person, an animal, or a natural feature, and may be at another place in time.

REVELATION
Making known something that has previously been unknown or kept a secret.

SACRIFICE
Giving something precious to a king, god, or deity, such as a treasured possession, food, or the life of an animal or a person, often in exchange for a need, such as to stop something bad from happening.

SEDER
A Jewish meal held on the first night of the Passover festival.

SHAMAN
A healer who tries to cure illness or problems by contacting the spirit world to drive away evil.

SHINTO
The ancient religion of Japan. Many gods, representing ancestors, places or the forces of nature, are worshipped at shrines marked by traditional archways.

SHRINE
A religious place of worship, or the tomb of a holy person.

SOUL
The spirit, or innermost part of a being, that is not physical.

SPIRIT
The soul of a person, often thought to survive the body after death. Some people widely believe that the spirit lives on forever, sometimes in another body or in another place.

SUPERNATURAL
Forces, happenings, or beings that cannot be explained by nature and science, and so are attributed to magic or the gods.

SUPERNOVA
An explosion faraway in space, when an old star blows up and dies. It usually lasts only a few days but is very bright and a new sight in the night sky.

SYNAGOGUE
A building where people belonging to the Jewish religion gather for prayers, ceremonies, services, teaching, and worship.

TIPI (TEPEE)
A cone- or pyramid-shaped dwelling made of long wooden poles covered with animal skins, often built by Native Americans, especially the Sioux.

TOTEM
The spirit of an animal, plant, object, natural phenomenon, or dead ancestor, which helps a group of people to carry out rituals in its honor.

TRADITION
The passing on of a culture of a group of people from old to young, including their customs, stories, history, and beliefs.

TRANCE
A sleeplike state when a person is unaware and unresponsive to what is happening to him or her, but may still be able to move about, speak or make noises.

UNIVERSE
Us, our world, our sun, the planets and stars, every atom, energy, space and time—everything that we are aware of.

WORSHIP
To give thanks, praise, and prayer to a god or gods.

ZEN
A type of Buddhism, popular in Japan. Followers believe meditation to be the best way to reach spiritual peace.

RELIGION

ACKNOWLEDGMENTS

Art Archive: Page 11 (t/r) National Library of Australia, 12 (c/l) Art Archive, 14 (t/r) Harper Collins Publishers, 15 (t/l) Art Archive, 16 (t/r) Victoria and Albert Museum London/Sally Chappell, (b/l) Art Archive, 17 (c/l) National Anthropological Museum Mexico/Dagli Orti, 19 (t/c) Dagli Orti, (c/l) National Anthropological Museum Mexico/Dagli Orti, (c/r) Musée des Arts Africains et Océaniens/ Dagli Orti, 24 (t/r) British Museum, 29 (t/l) United Society for Propagation of Gospel/Eileen Tweedy **Corbis:** Page 11 (c/r) Alison Wright, 15 (b/l) Paul Almasy, 21 (b/l) Lindsay Hebberd, (b/r) Sheldan Collins, 22 (c) Dean Conger, 25 (t/l) Lawrence Manning, 27 (b) Richard T. Nowitz, 29 (c/r) Daniel Lainé, (c/l) Jerry Cooke, 31 (t/r) Corbis, 32 (b) Adam Wolfitt, 35 (t) The Purcell Team

All other photographs are from:
MKP Archives; Corel Corporation; Photodisk

Other titles in this series:
**Art • Design • History of Culture • Literature
Music • Myths and Legends • Performing Arts**